Find MIND

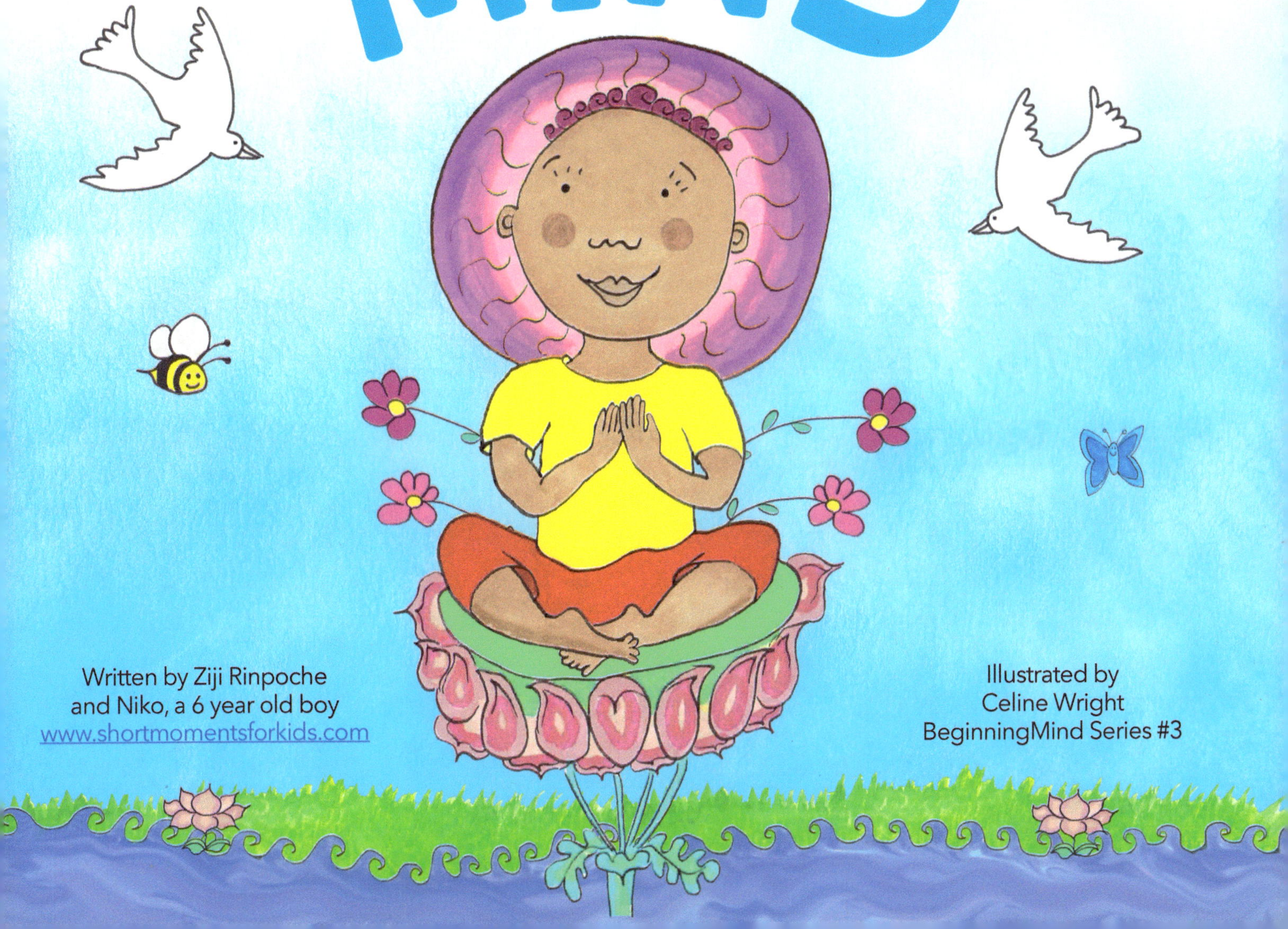

Written by Ziji Rinpoche
and Niko, a 6 year old boy
www.shortmomentsforkids.com

Illustrated by
Celine Wright
BeginningMind Series #3

Copyright © 2021 Short Moments for Kids
All rights reserved.

No part of this publication may be reproduced
or distributed in any form without prior
written consent from the publisher.

Text © 2021 Ziji Rinpoche
Illustrations and cover design © 2021 Celine Wright

Book #3 of the BeginningMind Series

Hardback ISBN: 978-1-9993537-7-3
Paperback ISBN: 978-1999353766
Ebook ISBN: 978-1-9993537-8-0

http://shortmomentsforkids.com

Short Moments of Strong Mind
for Kids

Dedicated to... you!

Practice strong mind when you have stormy feelings
because strong mind is always happy, calm
and has very powerful kindness.
Strong mind is always available to help you.
Strong mind belongs to you and no one can take it away!
It belongs to you!

Did we know how to name the parts of our body when we were a baby?

No! When we are a baby, we don't know anything.

then another step,
now we can walk all the time.

Now you are a big girl
or a big boy
and you can name
the parts of
your body too.

Being a big girl or a big boy
is very special
because you can learn
about your mind.

When you learn about the mind
you grow happier
and happier.

The way to best learn about your mind is called "meditation".

What do you need to know about the mind?

We need to know the mind is the only way to be happy.

Without the mind, we would not know how to be happy.

The mind tells your body what to do.

The mind tells your speech what to say.

So when you meditate, you learn

to be happy all of the time.

When you learn about the mind
through meditation,
you grow happier
and happier, and you are
more and more kind.

When you meditate
you learn happiness
and kindness and strength!

The greatest strength
is in the mind.
Just like the sky,

happiness and kindness
are everywhere
in the mind.

Happiness and kindness are like flowers in a field. When you meditate in short moments, repeated many times, like flowers spread in a field, your happiness and kindness and strength spread everywhere.

The author Ziji Rinpoche and her teacher Wangdor Rimpoche

Ziji Rinpoche loves to teach and write and her latest book is called 'When Surfing a Tsunami...' Ziji Rinpoche is the Dzogchen Lineage successor of Venerable Wangdor Rimpoche. Each metaphor and key instruction originate from Dzogchen teachings which were passed down from one teacher to another, like a chain of golden mountains. Wangdor Rimpoche asked Ziji Rinpoche to bring about the furtherance of Dzogchen within contemporary global culture. Ziji Rinpoche established the Short Moments online community for mutual support in gaining familiarity with the nature of mind. Through the Short Moments app, anyone can access profound and powerful Dzogchen teachings. Find out more on http://shortmoments.com

The illustrator Celine Wright

Celine loves to draw, empower children and tell stories. When she was introduced to the nature of mind by Ziji Rinpoche, she was awestruck at the power of mind, open like the sky, always clear and wise no matter the stormy feelings. She recognized she would have loved to learn about mind as a child. She was inspired to illustrate the teachings in children's books introducing strong mind to children. Combining her training in Fine Arts (BA), Performing Arts (MA), Dzogchen (Student of Ziji Rinpoche since 2007) and Early Years (Childminder), Celine now teaches Dzogchen for Kids, conducts book readings in schools and festivals and loves to illustrate new books at http://shortmomentsforkids.com

Happiness and kindness are like flowers in a field. When you meditate, in short moments repeated many times, like flowers spread in a field, your happiness and kindness and strength spread everywhere.

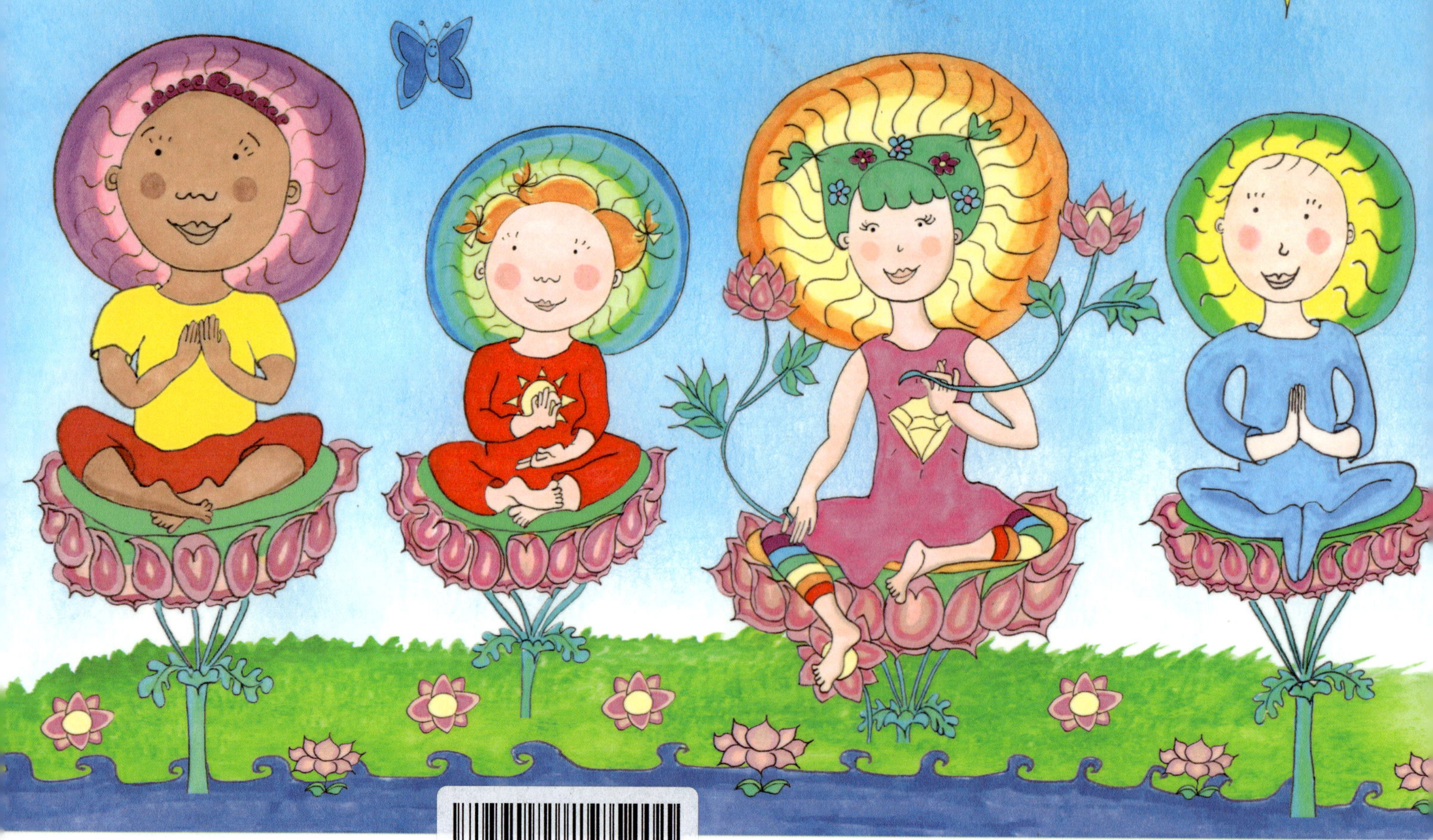

Short Moments of Strong Mind for Kids

Through the ShiningMind books, kids learn how to relax in mind to be happy and act with kindness and deep wisdom. The texts are for the children and adults of today and are written by Ziji Rinpoche, Dzogchen lineage successor of Wangdor Rimpoche.
www.shortmomentsforkids.com

ISBN 978-1-9993537-6-6